MW01617369

# Wild & Wonderful

## GOOSE & GAME

Helen Webber and Marie Woolsey,
authors of
*Blueberries & Polar Bears*
and
*Cranberries & Canada Geese,*
introduce their
Wild & Wonderful Series of Cookbooks with:

*Wild & Wonderful Blueberries*
*Wild & Wonderful Cranberries*
*Wild & Wonderful Goose & Game*

Helen Webber
&
Marie Woolsey

# *Wild & Wonderful* - GOOSE & GAME

by
Helen Webber & Marie Woolsey

First Printing – April 1998

Published by
Blueberries & Polar Bears Publishing
P.O. Box 304
Churchill, Manitoba
Canada   R0B 0E0

**Canadian Cataloguing in Publication Data**

Webber, Helen, 1947 –

      Wild & wonderful goose & game

      ISBN 1-894022-06-8

1. Cookery (Blueberries).    I. Woolsey, Marie, 1942 –
II. Title.

TX715.W43  1998        641.6'91        C98-920078-7

Cover Photograph by:
Ross (Hutch) Hutchinson, Hutchinson and Company
Calgary, Alberta

Designed, Printed and Produced in Canada by:
Centax Books,
   a Division of PrintWest Communications Ltd.
Publishing Director, Photo Designer & Food Stylist:
   Margo Embury
1150 Eighth Avenue, Regina, Saskatchewan,
         Canada  S4R 1C9
            (306) 525-2304   FAX: (306) 757-2439

# INTRODUCTION

Wild meat is becoming more and more popular across Canada, probably because it is guaranteed lean and free from hormones. Besides being a healthy alternative, it's delicious! Today it is offered in the best restaurants in Montreal, Toronto, Calgary and Vancouver and also sold in many butcher shops. But our purpose in writing this little book is in response to those many people who have wild game in their freezers and don't know what to do with it, as well as for those who are tired of the same old recipes and want to try something new. Most of these recipes have been used, many annually, at North Knife Lake Fishing Lodge and Dymond Lake Hunting Lodge, both owned and operated by Doug and Helen Webber. Other recipes have been given by family, friends and well-wishers who want to share what they've enjoyed and we are happy to co-operate.

We haven't included many recipes that call for ground meat, because our ground meat ends up in Spaghetti Sauce, Lasagne, Meat Loaf or soup and we use the same recipes that we would for ground beef.

We are happy to share with you our 30 years of experience, and we hope you will taste and enjoy!

Some of these recipes are from our other cookbooks, *Blueberries & Polar Bears* and *Cranberries & Canada Geese* and others were created especially for this book. Our goal is to provide the best possible range of Goose & Game recipes in a small affordable book designed especially for hunters and everyone who loves the flavor of goose and game.

**Dymond Lake Seasoning (DLS)** is used in many of our recipes. It is our own unique blend of herbs and spices. It contains no MSG. If you are unable to find DLS, substitute 1 tsp. (5 mL) seasoned pepper, 1 tsp. (5 mL) celery salt, 1 tbsp. (15 mL) dried parsley, ½ tsp. (2 mL) dried oregano, ½ tsp. (2 mL) dried basil, ½ tsp. (2 mL) dried thyme and salt to taste. To order Dymond Lake Seasoning, see page 47.

# "POLAR BEARS PREFER COKE"

I am sure that all of you have seen the advertising that Coca Cola has been doing with Polar Bears. Well, at Dymond Lake this fall we had proof that Polar Bears really do prefer Coke!

As is the custom, Stewart took Ron Nilsson and a friend from Utah out to their goose-hunting blind early in the morning while it was still dark. He set them up with their decoys and then headed off to another blind with some other hunters. Ron and his friend huddled down in their blind to wait for daylight and the first flight of geese. As daylight came, and the geese didn't arrive, they cracked open a couple of soft drinks to while away the time. (Ron chose a coke and his friend a rival brand.) Very suddenly their serene and carefree mood was interrupted by the unexpected approach of a mother and cub Polar Bear making a direct beeline for their blind. Ron and his friend made a hasty exit. There was no contest – if she wanted the blind she could have it!

Ron and his buddy arrived back at the lodge fairly excited, and after stopping to refuel (I think Ron had six cinnamon rolls) Doug and the hunters headed back to see if the bears were still in the blind. They were, so Doug used flares to scare them off. With fear and trepidation, Ron went into the blind to check out their precious equipment – Mama Bear hadn't even touched their backpacks which carried their lunches – but she had finished off Ron's coke! The can was punctured all over and rather squished as if she had been trying to squeeze out the last drop; and Ron has an unusual souvenir to remember a great hunting trip!

# TABLE OF CONTENTS

# AGING GOOSE AND GAME

We are often asked how to properly age wild game. Doug Webber has the answer to that.

"I am very particular about keeping the meat as clean as possible right from the first slit of the skinning knife to the last wrap of the butcher paper. The only other step in my butchering process is to hang the meat for 3 to 20 days – the length of time being determined by the cut of meat and the temperature of the cold room.

An average cold room temperature would be 40°F (4.4°C). I hang the ribs for only 3 days; the backbone with only an inch or so of rib I hang for a week; the front hangs for 3 days if it is to be ground up, and for 10 days if it is to be cut into steaks and roasts. The hind quarters hang for 20 days. During the hanging time, dry skin will form on the meat, and occasionally bits of mold form as well. Don't worry about the mold, it gets trimmed off with the dry skin.

I leave my steak meat in roast-size chunks and cut it just prior to cooking, after it has reached room temperature. It is more tender this way. I caution you, however, not to overcook a tender cut; even wild meat is best if the middle is rare to medium."

If you don't have aging facilities, leaving a piece of meat, covered, in the refrigerator for 4 to 7 days before cooking, will achieve the same results as hanging.

Thanks, Doug. He is also ready to credit Helen's cooking skills for the great taste of the wild meat.

# DUCK TASTE TEASER WITH BACON & WATER CHESTNUTS

*A long name for a treat that is simply good!*

| | | |
|---|---|---:|
| 1 cup | dry red wine | 250 mL |
| 2 | garlic cloves, minced, OR ½ tsp. (2 mL) garlic powder | 2 |
| 1 tbsp. | soy sauce | 15 mL |
| 6-8 | duck breasts OR 3-4 young goose breasts, cut into bite-sized pieces | 6-8 |
| 10 oz. | can sliced water chestnuts | 284 mL |
| 1 lb. | thinly sliced bacon strips, halved | 500 g |

1. Combine red wine, garlic and soy sauce in a large bowl. Add the duck pieces and marinate in the refrigerator for 8 hours or overnight.
2. Remove duck pieces from marinade; place a slice of water chestnut on each side; wrap with a bacon strip and secure with a wooden toothpick. They may be prepared ahead to this point, covered and refrigerated.
3. Roast at 350°F (180°C) for 25 to 30 minutes, until bacon is cooked. Serve hot!

**Makes 3 dozen**

*Freezing Hint: We remove the goose legs and breasts and pack them in 32-oz. (1 L) juice boxes; fill them with water so that the meat is completely covered and then freeze them. When you thaw them out there is no freezer burn and they taste as fresh as the day they were harvested.*

# GOOSE LIVER PÂTÉ

*The rich flavors of goose (or duck) livers make this creamy pâté irresistible.*

| | | |
|---|---|---|
| 2 tbsp. | butter | 30 mL |
| ½ cup | minced onion | 125 mL |
| ½ lb. | goose, duck OR chicken livers | 250 g |
| 1 cup | chicken stock | 250 mL |
| 4 | hard-cooked eggs | 4 |
| 1 cup | cooked tender goose meat | 250 mL |
| 2 tsp. | Dijon mustard | 10 mL |
| 6 drops | Tabasco sauce | 6 drops |
| 1 | garlic clove, crushed | 1 |
| 3 tbsp. | brandy | 45 mL |
| 2 tbsp. | lemon juice | 30 mL |
| | salt and pepper OR DLS* | |
| ⅔ cup | butter | 150 mL |
| ¼ lb. | cooked ham, finely diced | 125 g |
| ½ cup | pecans, finely ground | 125 mL |

1. Melt 2 tbsp. (30 mL) butter in a small frying pan. Add onion and sauté until soft.
2. Simmer livers in stock for 5 minutes. Drain.
3. In a blender or food processor, purée onion, livers, eggs, goose meat, mustard, Tabasco, garlic, brandy and lemon juice until absolutely smooth.
4. Force pâté through a sieve to remove all fibers. Season with salt and pepper or DLS*. Add remaining butter and purée until completely blended.
5. Add ham and mix, but do not purée. Refrigerate, covered, overnight.
6. For individual servings, line large muffin tins with paper baking cups. Fill cups with pâté. Refrigerate overnight. To serve, unmold individual pâtés on small plates. Top with pecans. If you wish, serve with Madeira Game Sauce, page 9.

**Serves 12 OR makes 12 small pâté molds**

* *Dymond Lake Seasoning, see note on page 3.*

# MADEIRA GAME SAUCE
## À LA REBHUN

*Dan Rebhun has hunted with us at Dymond Lake a number of times and we thank him for this recipe. It is terrific with any kind of wild game or with pâté.*

| | | |
|---|---|---|
| 14 oz. | can purple plums | 398 mL |
| 6 tbsp. | butter OR margarine | 90 mL |
| 1 tsp. | dried onion powder | 5 mL |
| 1 tsp. | dry mustard | 5 mL |
| 1 tsp. | ground ginger | 5 mL |
| 2 tbsp. | lemon juice | 30 mL |
| 2 tbsp. | chili sauce | 30 mL |
| ¼ cup | Madeira | 60 mL |

1. Remove the pits from the plums and purée the plums in a blender.
2. Combine the plums with the butter, onion, mustard, ginger, lemon juice and chili sauce in a heavy saucepan. Simmer for 30 minutes.
3. Add the wine; remove from the heat.
4. Serve over or under any wild game, or with Goose Liver Pâté, page 8.

**Makes about 2 cups (500 mL) of sauce**

\* *Madeira is a fortified wine from the Portuguese-owned island of Madeira. Port, sherry or red wine could be substituted for Madeira but the flavor will be different.*

*Helpful Hunting Hints: If you've never been lost, you've never been far from home.*

# GOOSE TIDBITS

*Still a favorite appetizer at Dymond Lake, after 20 years. Be sure to try the "hot" alternative.*

> **several goose breasts – YVGB\***
> **butter – the real thing!**
> **DLS\*\* OR seasoned pepper**
> **white vermouth**

1. Lay the goose breast flat on the cutting board and, with a sharp knife, slice along the top to make very thin slices.
2. Melt 2 tbsp. (30 mL) butter in a heavy frying pan over medium-high heat until it is sizzling.
3. Lay the goose slices in the frying pan and sprinkle liberally with DLS\*\*. They should brown quite quickly. If they do not, turn up the heat. When they are browned turn them over, sprinkle liberally again with DLS\*\*. Brown for about a minute.
4. Splash in about ¼ cup (60 mL) of white vermouth. Let the breasts simmer for about a minute.
5. Remove from pan and serve immediately, with toothpicks.

VARIATION: For **Hot Goose Tidbits**, replace the vermouth with either red or green Louisiana Hot Sauce OR other red pepper sauce.

\* *YVGB – Doug Webber's abbreviation for young, virgin goose boobies!*

\*\* *Dymond Lake Seasoning, see note on page 3.*

**Helpful Hunting Hints:** *Before you shoot at something a long way off, think about how long it will take you to get there.*

# DUCK À L'ORANGE

*Roast duck is a little tricky as you have to be careful that it does not dry out. The most important thing is to choose a young bird with a good layer of fat under its skin. Keeping the duck covered, basting and not overcooking are also important.*

| | | |
|---|---|---|
| 2 | plucked ducks OR 1 small plucked goose | 2 |
| 1 | medium onion, quartered | 1 |
| 2 tsp. | DLS* OR 1 tsp. (5 mL) salt and ½ tsp. (2 mL) pepper | 10 mL |

## À L'Orange Sauce

| | | |
|---|---|---|
| ¾ cup | currant jelly | 175 mL |
| ⅓ cup | white sugar | 75 mL |
| 1 tbsp. | grated orange rind | 15 mL |
| ¼ cup | port wine | 60 mL |
| ¼ cup | orange juice | 60 mL |
| ½ tsp. | salt | 2 mL |
| dash | cayenne pepper | dash |
| ¼ cup | lemon juice | 60 mL |

1. Prepare the birds. Place the onions in the bird cavity and sprinkle liberally with DLS*.
2. Place ducks or goose on sheets of aluminum foil that are large enough to completely wrap around the birds. Fold over and seal edges. (One sheet for each duck.)
3. Roast at 500°F (260°C) for 20 minutes (30 minutes for goose).
4. In a small saucepan, combine the jelly, sugar, orange rind, port, orange juice, salt and cayenne. Simmer for 5 minutes; remove from the heat and add the lemon juice.
5. Peel back the foil and brush the bird with the glaze. Reseal and return the bird to the oven until done, approximately 10 minutes (20 minutes for goose). Open the foil and use the juices to baste the bird again, at least once during the remaining baking time.

**Serves 3 to 4**

SERVE with Cranberry Sauce, Jelly or Chutney

*\* Dymond Lake Seasoning, see note on page 3.*

11

# WILD DUCK CASSEROLE

*A different method, combining roasting with baking, gives this casserole a wonderful flavor.*

| | | |
|---|---|---|
| 2 | ducks | 2 |
| | DLS* OR salt and pepper | |
| 2 tbsp. | butter, melted | 30 mL |
| 1 | medium turnip | 1 |
| 4 | bacon slices, cut into strips | 4 |
| 1½ cups | sliced OR quartered mushrooms OR 10. oz (284 mL) can | 375 mL |
| 2 tbsp. | brandy | 30 mL |
| ¼ cup | game-bird OR chicken stock | 60 mL |

1. Preheat oven to 450°F (230°C).
2. Rub ducks inside and out with DLS*. Brush with melted butter. Roast in the oven for 40 minutes, basting occasionally with butter. Remove birds and set aside on a plate.
3. Peel and cube turnip. Cook for 5 minutes in salted water, drain.
4. Fry bacon over medium-high heat. Once bacon starts to get crisp, add mushrooms and fry for a few minutes. Remove bacon and onions with a slotted spoon.
5. Lower oven to 375°F (190C). Cut off duck legs and breasts and place in an ovenproof 1½-quart (1.5 L) casserole. Pour brandy, stock and pan juices over meat; add turnip, bacon and mushrooms. Cover and place in the oven for 30 minutes, or until meat is tender.

**Serves 4**

* *Dymond Lake Seasoning, see note on page 3.*

**Helpful Hunting Hints: Don't hunt with people who make you nervous.**

# OVEN-ROASTED GOOSE

*We rarely choose to roast a wild goose as a whole bird since it tends to be somewhat dry, and unless you know that it is young, it can be tough. The following method is guaranteed moist, tender and tasty!*

|  | legs and breasts from 4 geese |  |
|---|---|---|
| ¼ cup | melted bacon drippings | 60 mL |
| ¼ cup | red Louisiana Hot Sauce OR other hot pepper sauce | 60 mL |
| 1 tbsp. | DLS* OR 1 tsp (5mL) each salt and seasoned pepper | 15 mL |

1. Place goose legs and breasts in a shallow roasting pan.
2. Drizzle with melted bacon drippings and Hot Sauce. Sprinkle with DLS*.
3. Place in a 450°F (230C) oven for 15 minutes to brown. Cover, turn oven down to 350°F (180C) and continue roasting for 2½ to 3 hours.
4. Thicken the pan juices with flour and water for a delicious gravy.

**Serves 6 to 8**

SERVING SUGGESTIONS: Use the leftover roasted goose in sandwiches. Remove the goose from the bones, chop the meat and add mayonnaise and seasonings.

*\* Dymond Lake Seasoning, see note on page 3.*

*Helpful Hunting Hints: Never brag about your shooting ability – especially before you start shooting!*

# JALEPEÑO GOOSE BREASTS SUPREME

*Among our guests at the Lodges, this is the undisputed favorite!*
*Could it be because they are as tender and tasty as a filet mignon?*

> **young goose breasts OR**
> **duck if they are large enough**
> **fresh garlic cloves, crushed**
> **soy sauce**
> **pickled jalepeño peppers and juice**
> **bacon drippings (no substitutes)**

1. Use approximately 3 breasts per person. Put a single layer of goose breasts in a glass or plastic dish.
2. Spread the breasts with crushed garlic and pour over ¼ to ½ cup (60 to 125 mL) soy sauce.
3. Add another layer of breasts, crushed garlic and soy sauce until all the breasts have been used. Be sure that the soy sauce almost covers the meat.
4. Refrigerate and allow to marinate for at least 8 hours or overnight.
5. An hour before serving, remove breasts from marinade and put a deep slit on each side of the breast with a small, sharp knife. Into each of these slits, stuff a small slice of pickled jalepeño pepper.
6. Now, get ready to barbecue! You will need a small dish of jalepeño juice from the pickle jar, a small dish of bacon drippings, a basting brush and a barbecue pre-heated to medium high. Barbecue the breasts for 4 to 6 minutes per side, basting often with jalepeño juice and bacon drippings. Test with a knife to ensure that they are still pink in the middle. Medium is perfection. Do not overcook

SERVING SUGGESTION: Serve whole breasts for a main course and slice leftover breasts thinly to use in sandwiches.

# SPICED CRANBERRY GOOSE BREASTS

*It's hard to beat the spicy goodness of this marinated and baked goose. It makes lots of sauce to serve over rice or noodles.*

| 8-12 | goose breasts (not too big) | 8-12 |
|---|---|---|
| 1 cup | whole berry cranberry sauce | 250 mL |
| 1 cup | cranberry juice | 250 mL |
| ½ cup | chopped red onion | 125 mL |
| 2 tbsp. | olive oil | 30 mL |
| 2 | garlic cloves, minced | 2 |
| 1 tbsp. | chopped fresh parsley OR 1 tsp. (5 mL) dry | 15 mL |
| 2 tsp. | cracked black pepper | 10 mL |
| 1 tsp. | salt | 5 mL |
| 1 tsp. | dried tarragon | 5 mL |
| 1 tsp. | curry powder | 5 mL |
| 1 tbsp. | cornstarch | 15 mL |
| 2 tbsp. | water | 30 mL |

1. Place goose parts in a plastic bag or sealable container. Combine all ingredients, except cornstarch and water, in a food processor and blend. Pour the marinade over the goose. Seal container and refrigerate overnight.
2. Place the goose with all the marinade in a casserole or roaster; cover and bake at 325°F (160°C) for 3 hours, or until tender.
3. Mix the cornstarch and water and add to the pan juices, stirring until thickened. Serve with rice or noodles.

**Serves 6 to 8**

*Helpful Hunting Hints: Don't brag about your equipment or skills. One is obvious, and the other soon will be.*

# MARITIME GOOSE

*Nova Scotia is home to an abundance of cranberries and wild geese – hence the name for this flavorful dish.*

| 6-8 | pieces of goose, (small breasts and/or legs) | 6-8 |
|---|---|---|
| ½ cup | flour | 125 mL |
| ¼ tsp. | salt | 1 mL |
| 4 tbsp. | butter OR margarine OR oil | 60 mL |
| 1½ cups | cranberries | 375 mL |
| ¾ cup | sugar | 175 mL |
| ¼ cup | chopped onion | 60 mL |
| ¾ cup | orange juice | 175 mL |
| 1 tsp. | grated orange rind | 5 mL |
| ¼ tsp. | each ginger and cinnamon | 1 mL |

1. Dredge goose pieces in a flour and salt mixture. Brown in butter, turning once.
2. Combine remaining ingredients in a saucepan. Bring to a boil and pour over the goose
3. Cover and cook slowly for about 40 to 60 minutes, until tender.

**Serves 4 to 6**

**Helpful Hunting Hints: Some people are luckier than others.**

# GOOSE À LA CHERRY SAUCE

*Long, slow cooking makes this recipe a good one for the big Canadas or older geese.*

| | | |
|---|---|---|
| 4 | large goose breasts | 4 |
| 1 cup | flour | 250 mL |
| | oil for browning | |
| 2 cups | beef stock | 50 mL |
| 2 tbsp. | A-1 OR HP sauce | 30 mL |
| ¼ cup | sherry | 60 mL |
| ⅛ tsp. | dried marjoram OR ½ tsp. (2 mL) fresh | 0.5 mL |
| 2 tsp. | DLS* OR 1 tsp. (5 mL) salt and ½ tsp. (2 mL) pepper | 10 mL |
| 2 | bay leaves | 2 |
| 2 tbsp. | cornstarch | 30 mL |
| 14 oz. | can pitted sweet cherries, drained, juice saved | 398 mL |
| 2 tbsp. | brandy | 30 mL |

1. Cut goose breasts into chunks, like stewing beef. Dredge in flour and brown in the oil in a Dutch oven. Remove the goose to a bowl.
2. To the drippings in the Dutch oven, add the beef stock, A-1 or HP sauce, sherry, marjoram, DLS* and bay leaves. Simmer for 2 to 3 minutes, add the goose, cover and cook in a 325°F (160C) oven for 2½ hours, or until goose is tender.
3. Mix the cornstarch with about ¼ cup (60 mL) of the cherry juice. Stir until smooth and then add the rest of the juice and the brandy.
4. Remove the pan from the oven and remove the meat. Add the cornstarch mixture and cook over medium heat until thickened and bubbly. Add the goose and simmer for 15 minutes. Add the cherries and remove the pan from the heat.

**Serves 8**

SERVING SUGGESTION: Serve with rice or pasta.

* *Dymond Lake Seasoning, see note on page 3.*

# MUSHROOM, WILD RICE AND GOOSE CASSEROLE

*A long-time favorite of Helen's daughter, Jeannie. Add a salad and some cranberry sauce and dinner is ready.*

| | | |
|---|---|---:|
| 2 | whole geese, cut in parts OR the equivalent in duck parts OR all legs | 2 |
| ¾ cup | butter OR margarine | 175 mL |
| 1 cup | chopped onion | 250 mL |
| 1 cup | chopped celery | 250 mL |
| 3 cups | sliced mushrooms OR 2, 10 oz. (284 mL) cans | 750 mL |
| 2 tsp. | DLS* OR 1 tsp. (5 mL.) salt and ½ tsp. (2 mL) pepper | 10 mL |
| ½ cup | flour | 125 mL |
| 3 cups | milk | 750 mL |
| 4 cups | cooked, wild rice** (1 cup raw) | 1 L |
| ¼ cup | broth from goose | 60 mL |

1. Cover the goose or duck parts with water and simmer until the meat falls off the bones, about 2 to 3 hours. Remove the meat, cool and dice. Save ¼ cup (60 mL) of broth.
2. Melt butter in a large Dutch oven, add onion, celery and mushrooms and cook until translucent. Add flour and stir until smooth. Slowly add the remaining ingredients.
3. Pour into a greased 3-quart (3 L) casserole and bake at 325°F (160°C) for 1 hour.

**Serves 4 to 6**

\* *Dymond Lake Seasoning, see note on page 3.*

\*\* *Wild rice has a unique and very special flavor. It expands more than long-grain rice, the usual ratio is 1 cup (250 mL) of wild rice to 3 cups (750 mL) of water. Cook for 35 to 45 minutes, until tender but not too soft. Try chicken stock instead of water for added flavor.*

# MUSHROOM GOOSE

*This was one of the original recipes used by Helen at the hunting lodge "back before the dawn of time". It is simple and very tasty.*

| | | |
|---|---|---|
| 1 cup | flour | 250 mL |
| 1 tsp. | DLS* OR ½ tsp. (2 mL) seasoned pepper | 5 mL |
| 1 | garlic clove, crushed (or ¼ tsp. [1 mL] garlic powder) | 1 |
| ½ tsp. | salt | 2 mL |
| | legs and breasts of 4 birds OR the equivalent | |
| | vegetable oil for frying | |
| 19 oz. | can mushroom soup | 540 mL |
| 10 oz. | can mushrooms with liquid | 284 mL |
| ½ cup | dry white wine | 125 mL |

1. Mix the first 4 ingredients together in a sturdy plastic bag. Shake the legs and breasts in the flour mixture.
2. Brown the goose pieces in ¼" (1 cm) vegetable oil in a frying pan OR place them on a greased baking sheet and bake them at 400°F (200°C) for 20 minutes, or until nicely browned.
3. Place the browned goose pieces in a roaster or baking dish.
4. Whisk the soup, mushrooms (with liquid) and wine together and pour over goose pieces.
5. Cover and bake for 3 hours at 325°F (160°C). Stir at least twice during baking. If sauce is too thick you can thin it with a little milk before serving.

**Serves 6**

* *Dymond Lake Seasoning, see note on page 3.*

***Helpful Hunting Hints:** Never criticize another man's dog – even if he asks you.*

# DYMOND LAKE GOOSE GUMBO

*When we decided to try making gumbo, neither of us knew quite what it was. Not to worry though, gumbo is what we call the thick mud along the mud flats of Hudson Bay, so we thought – okay, this has to be a thick stew. "Not so!" our deep-south guests told us when we added it to our Dymond Lake menu, "authentic gumbo is a very thin soup!" But they urged us not to change ours one bit, so we haven't and here it is!*

| | | |
|---|---|---|
| 8 | geese, breasts and legs from (or the equivalent) | 8 |
| 2 tbsp. | DLS* OR 2 tsp. (10 mL) seasoned salt and 1 tsp. (5 mL) pepper | 30 mL |
| 1 tsp. | cayenne pepper | 5mL |
| | Louisiana Hot Sauce OR Tabasco Sauce, to taste | |
| ¼ cup | bacon drippings, melted | 60 mL |
| 2 cups | bacon drippings | 500 mL |
| 2 cups | flour | 500 mL |
| 2 cups | finely diced celery | 500 mL |
| 2 cups | finely diced green pepper | 500 mL |
| 2½ cups | finely chopped onion | 625 mL |
| 3 | garlic cloves, crushed | 3 |
| 2 qts. | boiling water | 2 L |
| 1 | bunch green onions, chopped (optional) | 1 |

1. Place the goose parts in a shallow roasting pan. Sprinkle LIBERALLY with the DLS, cayenne and Hot Sauce. Drizzle over about ¼ cup (60 mL) melted bacon drippings.
2. Place the goose in a 400°F (200C) oven. Turn the pieces over after 20 minutes to brown the other side. Check after 20 more minutes and, if necessary, add some boiling water so that it will steam. We usually find that there is already enough liquid.
3. Cover and return to the oven at 325°F (160C) for 2 to 3 hours, or until the meat is falling off the leg bones.

# DYMOND LAKE GOOSE GUMBO

*continued*

4. Remove the goose from the oven and remove the meat from the pan. When it is cool enough to handle cut the meat into bite-sized pieces and set aside. Leave the juice in the pan for the next step.

5. Begin heating 2 cups (500mL) of bacon drippings in a large, heavy pot over medium heat. When the drippings are melted, add the flour and stir continuously, using a wire whisk. Do not let the flour stick or burn. Continue stirring and cooking until the roux** is the color of cocoa. You don't want it too pale but too dark gives a slightly burnt flavor.

6. When the roux has reached the proper colour, add the celery, green pepper, onions and garlic. Be sure you have on an oven mitt – the roux will bubble and steam when you throw in the vegetables. Cook, stirring often, until the vegetables are limp, about 15 minutes.

7. At this point, heat the reserved pan juices to boiling and add them slowly to the roux, stirring continuously to keep it smooth.

8. Next, add 4 cups (1 L) of boiling water, again stirring constantly to keep the roux smooth. Add another 3 to 4 cups boiling water to make the gumbo a nice, thick stew-like consistency.

9. Add the diced goose. Simmer until all the flavors have blended, at least 45 minutes. Taste and add salt, pepper and cayenne as needed. The flavor should be hot and spicy.

**Serves 12 or more**

SERVING SUGGESTION: Serve over a bed of rice, in a bowl. Top with chopped green onions, if desired.

\* *Dymond Lake Seasoning, see note on page 3.*

\*\* *ROUX: A cooked mixture of flour and fat, used as a flavoring and thickening agent in soups, stews and gravies.*

# GOOSE PIE

*This is one of the recipes our repeat customers insist on every year at the hunting lodge. Serve it with cranberry sauce and gravy. We save any leftover gravy from turkey, pork, beef or caribou, and freeze it to use later with our goose pie.*

| | | |
|---|---|---:|
| 2 | geese, legs and breasts of OR the equivalent in legs | 2 |
| ½ cup | chopped onions | 125 mL |
| 4 | beef bouillon cubes (4 tsp. [20 mL]) | 4 |
| 1 | garlic clove, minced | 1 |
| 1 tsp. | Worcestershire sauce | 5 mL |
| 2 tbsp. | DLS* | 30 mL |
| 2 cups | diced potatoes | 500 mL |
| 1 cup | diced carrots | 250 mL |
| ¼ cup | flour | 60 mL |
| 1 cup | cold water | 250 mL |
| | pastry for a 10" (25 cm), 2-crust pie, see page 23 | |

1. Place the first 6 ingredients in a large Dutch oven and cover with water. Simmer until the meat falls off the leg bones, about 3 to 4 hours.
2. Let cool, remove the meat from the bones. Discard any meat that is still tough. That bird was too old! Chop up the breasts if they have not already fallen apart.
3. Return the meat to the broth in the Dutch oven and add the vegetables. Barely cover with water. Cook until the vegetables are tender, about 30 minutes. Taste to check seasoning and add a little salt or more DLS* to taste.
4. Blend the flour into the cold water, shaking it in a jar or using a hand blender. Stir into the pie filling; simmer and stir for about 2 minutes.

5. Pour the filling into the uncooked pie shell. Cover with top crust; cut slits to allow the steam to escape and bake at 425°F (220°C) for 10 minutes. Lower heat to 375°F (190°C) and bake for an additional 40 minutes.

**Serves 4 to 6. This freezes well, baked or unbaked.**

* *For Dymond Lake Seasoning, see page 3.*

# FLAKY PASTRY

| | | |
|---|---|---|
| 1¾ cups | all-purpose flour | 425 mL |
| ¾ tsp. | salt | 4 mL |
| ⅓ lb. | lard (⅔ cup [150 mL]) | 150 g |
| 1 | egg yolk | 1 |
| 1½ tsp. | vinegar | 7 mL |
| | cold water | |

1. Combine the flour and salt; cut in the lard with a pastry blender or 2 knives until crumbly. Place egg yolk into a ⅓ cup (75 mL) measuring cup. Add vinegar and whisk with a fork. Fill to the top with cold water. Add to the flour mixture and mix with a fork until it just clings together and pulls away from the side of the bowl.

2. Divide dough in half; roll each portion out on a lightly floured surface, rolling from the center to the outside edge to keep the dough round. If the dough is sticky, sprinkle a little more flour on your rolling surface.

**Makes enough pastry for 1, 9" (23 cm) or 10" (25 cm), 2-crust pie or 2 pie shells.**

# LOOED GOOSE

*Excellent flavor and easy preparation are the keys to this Chinese recipe which only SOUNDS naughty. "Looing" refers to simmering in a soy-based sauce, resulting in meat that is tender and moist.*

LOOING SAUCE

| | | |
|---|---|---|
| 3 cups | soy sauce | 750 mL |
| ½ cup | sugar | 125 mL |
| ½ cup | dry sherry OR rice wine | 125 mL |
| 6 slices | fresh ginger | 6 slices |
| 2 | star anise, whole | 2 |
| 3 qts. | water | 3 L |
| 8 | goose legs and/or breasts (preferably young) | 8 |

1. Place all of the ingredients for the sauce in a large pot and bring to a boil.
2. Add the goose pieces and add additional water just so that the pieces are barely covered. Bring to a boil, cover, and simmer gently for 30 minutes.
3. Remove the pot from the heat, but leave covered. Allow the meat to sit for another hour in the looing sauce.
4. Reheat and serve with rice.

NOTE: If you suspect the goose was not a young bird, increase the simmering time accordingly or cut the breast meat into smaller pieces.

**Helpful Hunting Hints: The best shooting instructor is a case of shells.**

24

# GOOSE STIR-FRY

*Serve this to guests or your family and they will have a hard time believing it is not a beef stir-fry! Use your favorite vegetables.*

| | | |
|---|---|---|
| 6 | medium goose breasts | 6 |
| 1 cup | soy sauce | 250 mL |
| 2 | garlic cloves, crushed | 2 |
| | vegetable oil | |
| 1 cup | chunked onions | 250 mL |
| ½ cup | chunked celery | 125 mL |
| 1 cup | broccoli | 250 mL |
| 1 cup | cauliflower florets | 250 mL |
| 1 | green pepper, cut in strips | 1 |
| 1 cup | diagonally cut carrots | 250 mL |
| 1 cup | sliced mushrooms | 250 mL |
| 2 tbsp. | fresh ginger root, chopped (optional) | 30 mL |
| 3 tbsp. | cornstarch | 45 mL |
| ½ cup | cold water | 125 mL |
| | DLS* OR salt and pepper to taste | |

1. Cut goose breasts into long thin strips; place in a glass or plastic bowl. Add soy sauce and crushed garlic. Stir well; cover; marinate in the refrigerator for 6 to 8 hours.
2. Remove goose from marinade; drain; reserve marinade.
3. Heat 2 tbsp. (30 mL) oil in a large frying pan or wok. Add ½ the goose; stir-fry over medium-high, until nicely browned. Remove from the pan; add a bit more oil; fry the second batch of goose. Remove from the pan.
3. Wipe out the pan; add 2 tbsp. (30 mL) oil. Stir-fry vegetables and ginger until tender-crisp, about 7 minutes.
5. Return the goose to the pan and add the reserved marinade. Cook over medium heat until just simmering.
6. Mix the cornstarch with the water and add to the saucepan. Stir gently until the sauce thickens and loses its cloudiness. Season to taste.

**Serves 6**

SERVING SUGGESTION: Serve over noodles or rice.

*\* Dymond Lake Seasoning, see note on page 3.*

# WILD GAME MEATBALLS WITH CRANBERRY DIP OR SAUCE

*Serve these tasty meatballs as an hors d'oeuvre with a dip, OR make larger meatballs and serve them as a main course, in the sauce. Either way, enjoy the tart goodness of cranberries in the meat!*

| | | |
|---|---|---|
| 1½ lbs. | ground moose, caribou, deer or any available wild game | 750 g |
| 2 | eggs | 2 |
| ½ cup | cranberries | 125 mL |
| 1 tbsp. | soy sauce | 15 mL |
| 10 oz. | water chestnuts, drained and chopped | 284 mL |
| 1 tsp. | DLS* OR salt and pepper to taste | 5 mL |
| ½ cup | minced onion | 125 mL |
| ¼ cup | butter OR margarine | 60 mL |

1. Combine ground meat, eggs, cranberries, soy sauce, water chestnuts, salt, pepper and onion. Shape into tiny balls.
2. Place the meatballs on a greased baking sheet with sides and brown them at 350°F (180°C) for 10 minutes, or until cooked through.
3. Spear the meatballs with toothpicks and serve with Cranberry Dip, page 27.

**Makes about 100 cocktail-size meatballs**

VARIATION: For a main course dish, make slightly larger meatballs. Increase the baking time to 15 minutes. Place the meatballs in a casserole and pour the warm Cranberry Sauce, page 27, over. Serve with steamed rice.

**Makes about 50 meatballs**

* *Dymond Lake Seasoning, see page 3.*

# CRANBERRY DIP OR SAUCE

| 3 tbsp. | cornstarch | 45 mL |
| 2 cups | cranberry juice | 500 mL |
| ¼ cup | cider OR cranberry vinegar | 60 mL |
| ¼ cup | sugar | 60 mL |
| ½ tsp. | salt | 2 mL |
| 2 | chicken bouillon cubes | 2 |

Measure the cornstarch into a saucepan. Blend some cranberry juice with the cornstarch. Add the remaining juice and the vinegar, sugar, salt and bouillon cubes to the saucepan. Cook, stirring constantly, until the sauce is smooth and has thickened.

**Makes about 2 cups (500 mL) of dip**

*Rules for northern survival*
  *(From Rev. Dale Kuipers, Thompson, MB)*

*Watch not the northern lights while splitting wood,*
*A woodsman with three toes is not much good.*

*Rotten ice will give no quarter*
*Thus far, only one man walked on water.*

*A compass is a joke, we all agree,*
*But minus it, some folk have found eternity.*

*Only fools shoot at shapes and sounds,*
*Be sure thy prey with antlered brow abounds.*

*Pray for good weather, then for the worst prepare,*
*A cruel day oft comes, that first was promised fair.*

*Tell friends where thy trail may be found,*
*Lest thy departure with perplexity abound.*

# WILD MEATBALL TASTE TEASERS WITH FRUIT SAUCE

*This is a popular hors d'oeuvre whether you use wild meat or not!*

| | | |
|---|---|---|
| 2 lbs. | ground caribou, moose, deer OR elk | 1 kg |
| 3 tbsp. | soy sauce | 45 mL |
| 1 tbsp. | brown sugar | 15 mL |
| 10 oz. | can water chestnuts, finely chopped | 284 g |
| ½ cup | finely chopped onion | 125 mL |
| 1 tsp. | dried parsley flakes OR 1 tbsp. (15 mL) chopped fresh parsley | 5 mL |
| 2 | garlic cloves, minced | 2 |

1. Mix all of the ingredients together in a large bowl.
2. Shape the meat mixture into bite-sized balls.
3. Place the meatballs on a greased baking sheet with sides and bake at 375°F (190°C) for 10 to 15 minutes.

**Makes 4 dozen meatballs (approximately)**

NOTE: If it is more convenient, make the meatballs ahead of time. Reheat at 400°F (200°C) for 5 minutes.

## FRUIT SAUCE

| | | |
|---|---|---|
| 3 tbsp. | cider vinegar | 45 mL |
| 1 cup | apricot OR peach jam | 250 mL |
| ¼ tsp. | paprika | 1 mL |

Combine all of the ingredients and pour into a small glass dish. Surround with meatballs.

VARIATIONS: The cider vinegar makes a delicious tangy sauce. If you want to add even more tang and some heat, add a dash or 2 of cayenne pepper or hot sauce.

# GAVIN'S CARIBOU STRIPS

*This hors d'oeuvre, created by Helen's brother-in-law, Gavin Lawrie, is a winner. It has even been served to the Lieutenant Governor of Manitoba, and prepared for H.R.H. Prince Charles.*

### GARLICKY WINE MARINADE

| | | |
|---|---|---|
| 2 cups | dry red wine | 500 mL |
| 2 | garlic cloves, crushed | 2 |
| 2 tbsp. | soy sauce | 30 mL |
| ½ tsp. | dry mustard | 2 mL |
| | | |
| 2 lbs. | caribou strips, approx ½ x 2½" (1 x 6 cm) | 1 kg |
| 1 cup | flour | 250 mL |
| 2 tsp. | DLS* OR 1 tsp. (5 mL) each of seasoned salt and pepper | 10 mL |
| ¼ cup | vegetable oil | 60 mL |
| 2 tbsp. | butter OR margarine | 30 mL |

1. Combine all of the marinade ingredients and add the caribou strips. Marinate in the refrigerator for 8 hours or overnight.
2. Mix the flour and seasoning. Dredge** the drained caribou strips in the flour and sauté*** in the oil and butter, a handful at a time, until nicely browned. You may have to add more oil and butter.
3. Serve the strips with wooden toothpicks for easy handling.

**Makes 8 dozen strips**

SERVING SUGGESTIONS: Serve with ¼ cup (60 mL) of your favorite barbecue sauce mixed with ¼ cup (60 mL) of peach or apricot jam.

*\* Dymond Lake Seasoning, see note on page 3.*
*\*\* DREDGE: To shake in flour until completely coated.*
*\*\*\* SAUTÉ: To fry quickly, stirring constantly over high heat to seal in the juices.*

# MOOSE JERKY

*Thanks to Garry Webber for these 2 versions of Jerky. Take your choice or try them both and enjoy!*

### Onion Garlic Marinade:

| | | |
|---|---|---|
| ¼ cup | Worcestershire sauce | 60 mL |
| ¼ cup | Maggi Seasoning* | 60 mL |
| 2 tbsp. | soy sauce | 30 mL |
| 1 | garlic clove, crushed OR ½ tsp. (2 mL) garlic powder | 1 |
| ½ tsp. | onion salt | 2 mL |
| ¾ tsp. | DLS** | 3 mL |
| ¼ tsp. | cayenne OR more to taste | 1 mL |
| ½ tsp. | pepper | 2 mL |
| 2 tbsp. | brown sugar | 30 mL |

### OR Honey Ginger Marinade:

| | | |
|---|---|---|
| ¼ cup | Worcestershire sauce | 60 mL |
| ¼ cup | Maggi Seasoning* | 60 mL |
| ¼ cup | soy sauce | 60 mL |
| 1 tsp. | ground ginger OR 1 tbsp. (15 mL) grated fresh ginger | 5 mL |
| ¾ tsp. | DLS** | 3 mL |
| 1 | garlic clove, crushed OR 1 tsp. (5 mL) garlic powder | 1 |
| ½ tsp. | cayenne OR more to taste | 2 mL |
| ½ tsp. | pepper | 2 mL |
| ½ tsp. | celery salt | 2 mL |
| 3 tbsp. | brown sugar | 45 mL |
| 2 tbsp. | liquid honey (or more) | 30 mL |
| | | |
| 3½ lbs. | moose (or other wild meat) sliced very thinly*** | 1.75 g |

1. Combine all ingredients from the marinade of your choice. Marinate the meat in the refrigerator for 24 hours.
2. Lay waxed paper on an oven rack. Place pieces of meat on the waxed paper in a single layer. Bake at 150°F (65°C) for 4 to 7 hours with the door open a crack. (Place a wedge in the door, if necessary.)

*\* A liquid seasoning available at most grocery stores.*
*\*\* Dymond Lake Seasoning, see note on page 3.*
*\*\*\* Ask your butcher to do this for you.*

30

# RACK OF CARIBOU

*This entrée got a standing ovation at a dinner given for 100 people. Many of the seasoned northerners said they had never tasted such good caribou. This surprisingly easy recipe almost melts in your mouth. Be sure to try it with other wild meats, too.*

| | | |
|---|---|---|
| 2 | garlic cloves, crushed | 2 |
| 2 | racks* caribou, deer OR antelope | 2 |
| | DLS** OR salt and pepper | |
| 2 tbsp. | cooking oil | 30 mL |
| 2 tbsp. | butter OR margarine | 30 mL |
| ½ lb. | salt pork, cut in strips OR bacon | 250 g |
| 1½ oz. | pkg. onion soup mix | 40 g |
| 1 cup | beef stock | 250 mL |
| ½ cup | water | 125 mL |
| 1½ cups | sliced mushrooms, OR 10 oz. (284 mL) can | 375 mL |

1. Rub the crushed garlic clove on both sides of the racks and sprinkle liberally with the DLS**.
2. Heat the oil, butter and a small chunk of the salt pork in a heavy frying pan. Brown the racks on both sides in the oil mixture.
3. Remove the racks to a shallow baking pan. Lay strips of salt pork over them. Set the frying pan aside and reserve drippings in it.
4. Roast the racks in a 350°F (180C) oven for approximately 45 to 60 minutes, until they have reached the desired doneness. Medium to medium rare is best.
5. Remove racks from the pan; cut in half; place on a serving platter and keep warm.
6. To the frying pan used for browning, add the drippings from the baking pan, the onion soup mix, beef stock, water and mushrooms. Bring to a boil and simmer for 5 minutes.
7. Pour a small amount of the pan gravy over the racks. Serve the rest in a gravy boat.

\* *A rack is a portion of the rib section, usually containing about 8 ribs.*

\*\* *Dymond Lake Seasoning, see note on page 3.*

31

# ROAST BEAST WITH MUSHROOMS AU JUS

*Whenever we are sure we have a good cut of wild meat, right off the hoof, or well aged, we treat it like a good Prime Rib. (Loins of moose, hips of caribou, use your best judgement.) We never cook it more than medium, it makes great gravy, and you should see those hunters dig into it. It also makes great sandwiches.*

| | | |
|---|---|---|
| **8-10 lb.** | **prime beast** | **3.5-4.5 kg** |
| | **fresh garlic, crushed** | |
| | **DLS\*** | |

1. Bring the roast to room temperature and preheat the oven to 425°F (220°C)
2. Place the roast in a large roasting pan; rub crushed garlic liberally over the top and sides, then sprinkle liberally with Dymond Lake Seasoning\*.
3. Roast, uncovered, for 15 minutes. Reduce the temperature to 325°F (160°C) and continue to roast 20 minutes per pound for rare, 25 minutes per pound for medium and 30 minutes per pound for well. (We remove the roast from the oven when the internal temperature reaches 130°F [53°C].)
4. Remove the roast from the roaster; let it rest for 10 minutes while you prepare the Mushroom Au Jus, below.

\* *For Dymond Lake Seasoning, see note on page 3.*

## MUSHROOMS AU JUS

| | | |
|---|---|---|
| **1½ oz.** | **pkg. onion soup mix** | **40 g** |
| **10 oz.** | **can beef consommé (OR equivalent in stock)** | **284 mL** |
| **10 oz.** | **can sliced mushrooms, undrained** | **284 mL** |
| **2 cups** | **water** | **500 mL** |

Add all of the ingredients to the pan juices in the roaster. Simmer on low while you carve the beast!

# SWEET 'N' SOUR CARIBOU STEAKS

*Try this with any wild meat that is native to your area.*

| | | |
|---|---|---|
| 8 | caribou steaks | 8 |
| 3 tbsp. | olive OR vegetable oil | 45 mL |

SWEET 'N' SOUR SAUCE

| | | |
|---|---|---|
| 2 tsp. | DLS* OR 1 tsp. (5 mL.) salt and ½ tsp. (2 mL) pepper | 10 mL |
| 1½ cups | brown sugar | 375 mL |
| 2 tsp. | prepared mustard | 10 mL |
| 2 tbsp. | vinegar | 30 mL |

1. Brown the meat in the oil in a heavy frying pan over medium-high heat.
2. To make the sauce, combine the DLS*, brown sugar, mustard and vinegar.
3. Place the steaks in an ovenproof casserole or roaster. If the steaks don't fit in a single layer, just be sure to put sauce between the layers as well as on top of the steaks, otherwise, pour the sauce over the steaks.
4. Cover and roast at 350°F (180°C) for 1 hour. You may have to increase cooking time according to the cut and the type of wild meat. Test for doneness.

**Serves 8**

\* *Dymond Lake Seasoning, see note on page 3.*

*Helpful Hunting Hints: Always ask your guide to repeat the directions about where you'll meet later. Twice!*

# PEPPER PIE AU GRATIN

*Peppers and cheese give an added burst of flavor to this old classic. It freezes well and is handy to have when company comes for the weekend.*

| | | |
|---|---|---|
| 2 lbs. | potatoes, (approx. 4 large), peeled and cut into eighths | 1 kg |
| 2 tbsp. | vegetable oil | 30 mL |
| ¾ cup | chopped onion | 175 mL |
| 2 | garlic cloves, minced | 2 |
| 1 cup | sliced fresh mushrooms OR 14 oz. (398 mL) can | 250 mL |
| 1½ lbs. | ground caribou, moose OR other wild meat | 750 g |
| 1 cup | beef stock | 250 mL |
| 2 tbsp. | tomato paste | 30 mL |
| 1 tsp. | dry mustard | 5 mL |
| ½ tsp. | thyme leaves | 2 mL |
| 1 tbsp. | Worcestershire sauce | 15 mL |
| 2 tsp. | DLS* (or 1 tsp. [5 mL] salt and ½ tsp. [2 mL] pepper) | 10 mL |
| 14 oz. | can kernel corn | 398 mL |
| 1 tbsp. | cooking oil | 15 mL |
| 1 cup | diced pepper, red, green OR yellow OR mixture | 250 mL |
| ⅓ cup | milk | 75 mL |
| 2 | eggs | 2 |
| ½ tsp. | salt | 2 mL |
| ⅛ tsp. | pepper | 0.5 mL |
| 1 cup | grated medium Cheddar cheese | 250 mL |

1. Put the potatoes on to boil in lightly salted water.
2. Heat 2 tbsp. (30 mL) of oil in a heavy frying pan over medium heat. Add the onions and garlic and sauté until the onions begin to soften. Add the mushrooms and continue to cook until the mushrooms are golden. Transfer to an 8-cup (2 L) shallow casserole.
3. In the same pan, cook the ground meat until it is cooked through. Drain and add to the onion mixture.

# PEPPER PIE AU GRATIN

*continued*

4. Now add the beef stock, tomato paste, dry mustard, thyme, Worcestershire sauce and DLS* to the frying pan. Bring to a boil. Add to the meat mixture, mixing well.
5. Spread the drained corn over the meat mixture.
6. To the frying pan, add 1 tbsp. of oil and the peppers and sauté over medium heat for 2 to 3 minutes. Spread over the corn.
7. When the potatoes are tender, remove from the heat and drain. Add the milk, eggs, salt and pepper. Beat until light and fluffy. Stir in the grated cheese and spread over the peppers.
8. Bake, uncovered, at 425°F (220°C) for 15 minutes. Lower the oven temperature to 350°F (180°C) and continue to bake for 20 minutes longer, until the top is golden brown.

**Serves 6 to 8**

NOTE: The casserole may be made ahead and refrigerated. Add 15 minutes to the baking time. The casserole may also be frozen. Thaw before baking.

* *Dymond Lake Seasoning, see note on page 3.*

***Helpful Hunting Hints: Beautiful guns don't necessarily shoot better than plain ones, but they always seem to.***

# HUNTER'S PIE

*Serve this savory pie with chili sauce, creamy coleslaw and crusty rolls, then be ready to serve seconds.*

| | | |
|---|---|---|
| 1 lb. | moose, caribou, venison OR elk, cut into ¾" (2 cm) cubes | 500 g |
| | beef stock (to cover meat) | |
| ½ cup | chopped onion | 125 mL |
| ¼ cup | chopped celery | 60 mL |
| 1 | garlic clove, minced | 1 |
| 1 tbsp. | Worcestershire sauce | 15 mL |
| 1 tbsp. | DLS* OR see note on page 3 | 15 mL |
| 1 | bay leaf | 1 |
| 2 cups | diced potatoes | 500 mL |
| 1 cup | sliced carrots | 250 mL |
| ½ cup | diced turnip | 125 mL |
| 1½ cups | sliced mushrooms OR 10 oz. (284 mL) can | 375 mL |
| ¼ cup | flour | 60 mL |
| ¾ cup | cold water | 175 mL |
| | pastry for a 2-crust pie, see page 23 | |

1. Cover the meat with beef stock and bring to a boil. Add the onion, celery, garlic, Worcestershire sauce, DLS* and bay leaf. Simmer for 1 to 2 hours, or until tender. This will vary with the cut of meat.
2. Add the vegetables and continue to simmer until they are tender. Remove the bay leaf.
3. Blend the flour into the cold water, shaking it in a jar or using a hand blender, until smooth. Stir enough into the pie filling to thicken it. Simmer for 2 minutes.
4. Pour filling into the uncooked pie shell; cover with the top crust. Cut slits to vent steam and bake at 425°F (220°C) for 10 minutes; lower temperature to 350°F (180°C); bake for an additional 40 to 50 minutes, until the crust is browned and the filling is bubbly.

**Serves 2 to 4 hungry hunters or a family of 4 to 6.**

* *Dymond Lake Seasoning, see note on page 3.*

# HUNTER'S STEW

*Is there a nicer welcome for a weary hunter returning from a day in the field than the aroma of a rich stew simmering on the stove?*

| | | |
|---|---|---|
| ¼ cup | flour | 60 mL |
| 2 tsp. | DLS* OR 1 tsp. (5 mL) salt and 1 tsp. (5 mL) seasoned pepper | 10 mL |
| 2 lbs. | stewing meat cut in 1" (2.5 cm) cubes (use the wild meat of your choice) | 1 kg |
| 3 strips | bacon, diced | 3 strips |
| 2 | garlic cloves, minced | 2 |
| | beef stock to cover | |
| 1 cup | dry red wine | 250 mL |
| 2 tbsp. | Worcestershire sauce | 30 mL |
| ½ tsp. | thyme | 2 mL |
| 1 tsp. | oregano | 5 mL |
| 1 | bay leaf | 1 |
| 1½ cup | sliced OR chunked onions | 375 mL |
| ½ cup | sliced celery | 125 mL |
| 3 cups | quartered potatoes | 750 mL |
| 2 cups | carrots, in 1" (2.5 cm) chunks | 500 mL |
| ¼ cup | flour | 60 mL |
| ¾ cup | water | 175 mL |

1. Mix the flour and DLS* in a heavy plastic bag or bowl. Toss the meat cubes in the flour and set aside.
2. Cook the bacon until crisp in a heavy Dutch oven or crock pot. Add meat cubes and garlic. Cook over medium heat until browned, stirring occasionally. Add a little oil if needed. Add the stock, wine, Worcestershire, thyme, oregano and bay leaf. Bring to a boil; reduce to simmer; cover. Simmer for 1 to 1½ hours, until the meat is almost tender.
3. Add the onions, celery, potatoes and carrots. Cover and cook until the vegetables are tender, 30 to 40 minutes. Remove the bay leaf. Season to taste.
4. Mix the flour and cold water until smooth. Add enough to the stew to thicken to your liking. Simmer for 2 to 3 minutes.

**Serves 6 to 8**

*\* Dymond Lake Seasoning, see note on page 3.*

# RED WINE AND
# GARLIC MOOSE ROAST

*Start the night before with the marinade, but let this roast slow cook all day, then come home to a wonderful aroma.*

| 4-6 lb. | moose roast OR caribou OR elk | 1.8-2.5 kg |
|---|---|---|

**RED WINE GARLIC MARINADE**

| ½ cup | red wine vinegar | 125 mL |
|---|---|---|
| 2 | garlic cloves, crushed | 2 |
| 2 tbsp. | salt | 30 mL |
| 1 cup | dry red wine | 250 mL |
| | cold water | |

| ½ cup | flour | 125 mL |
|---|---|---|
| 1 tbsp. | DLS* OR 1 tsp. (5 mL) salt and ½ tsp. (2 mL) pepper | 15 mL |

**RED WINE GARLIC TOMATO SAUCE**

| 2 | garlic cloves, crushed | 2 |
|---|---|---|
| 2 tbsp. | brown sugar | 30 mL |
| 1 tsp. | Dijon OR American mustard | 5 mL |
| 1 tbsp. | Worcestershire sauce | 15 mL |
| ¼ cup | red wine vinegar OR lemon juice | 60 mL |
| 1 cup | dry red wine | 250 mL |
| 1 | large onion, sliced | 1 |
| 14 oz. | can tomatoes, crushed OR diced | 398 mL |

1. Place the roast in a plastic bag or container that allows the roast to be covered with the marinade. Combine vinegar, garlic, salt and wine. Add water to completely cover the roast. Marinate in the refrigerator overnight.
2. Mix the flour and DLS*. Remove the roast from the marinade and roll it in the flour mixture. Brown the roast in oil in a heavy frying pan over medium-high heat, then place it in a slow cooker or heavy roaster.
3. Mix the remaining ingredients and pour over the roast. Cover and cook on low in a slow cooker for 10 to 12 hours, or in the oven at 250°F (120°C) for 6 hours.

**Serves 8 to 10**

38

*\* Dymond Lake Seasoning, see note on page 3.*

# MOOSE POT ROAST – 2 WAYS !

*This makes a dandy hot moose sandwich. Pile the meat on a crusty roll and serve au jus, with bowls of the unthickened natural juices for dipping.*

| | | |
|---|---|---|
| 4 lbs. | moose OR caribou roast (one of the tougher cuts) | 1.8 kg |

### ONION BEEF BROTH POT ROAST

| | | |
|---|---|---|
| 1½ oz. | onion soup mix (1 envelope) | 40 g |
| 2 x 10 oz. | cans beef consommé | 2 x 284 mL |
| 2 x 10 oz. | cans water | 2 x 284 mL |

1. Place the roast in a roaster and sprinkle with the onion soup mix. Add consommé and water.
2. Cover the roast and cook at 275°F (140°C) for 5 hours.
3. Slice the roast (if it hasn't fallen apart already) and serve it on split crusty rolls with the juice from the pan for dipping.

**Serves 10 to 12**

VARIATIONS: Thicken the pan juices with flour and water to make gravy.

### MUSHROOM ONION POT ROAST

| | | |
|---|---|---|
| 1½ oz. | onion soup mix | 40 g |
| 2 x 10 oz. | cans mushroom soup | 2 x 284 mL |

Combine the onion soup mix with the mushroom soup. Pour over the roast in a roaster. Roast, covered, as above. Thin the gravy with water, if necessary, before serving.

NOTE: Both methods work well with goose breasts, too!

# MOOSE STROGANOFF

*You can use wild meat in almost anything that calls for beef. This is one we like a lot.*

| | | |
|---|---|---|
| 2 lbs. | moose sirloin steak | 1 kg |
| ¼ cup | flour | 60 mL |
| ¼ cup | vegetable oil | 60 mL |
| 1 | large onion, thinly sliced | 1 |
| 1½ cups | sliced mushrooms OR 10 oz. (284 mL) can | 375 mL |
| 2 tbsp. | flour | 30 mL |
| 1 cup | beef stock | 250 mL |
| 2 tbsp. | ketchup | 30 mL |
| 1 tbsp. | Worcestershire sauce | 15 mL |
| ½ tsp. | dry mustard | 2 mL |
| 2 tsp. | DLS* OR 1 tsp. (5 mL) salt and ½ tsp. (2 mL) pepper OR more to taste | 10 mL |
| 1 cup | sour cream | 250 mL |
| 3 tbsp. | sherry (optional) | 45 mL |

1. Dredge the steak strips in flour.
2. Heat oil in a heavy frying pan. Add the steak strips in batches and sauté, turning to brown on all sides. Remove steak strips and keep warm.
3. Return all of the meat to the frying pan; add onions and mushrooms and cook over medium heat until tender. Remove the meat and onions from the pan.
4. Blend in the flour, stock, ketchup, Worcestershire, mustard and DLS*, stirring constantly until smooth and thickened.
5. Return the meat mixture to the pan. Add the sour cream and sherry. Heat thoroughly but do not boil.

**Serves 6 to 8**

*\* Dymond Lake Seasoning, see note on page 3.*

# CHICKEN-FRIED MOOSE

*This dish is reminiscent of that deep-south dish – Chicken-Fried Steak. We find it is also very tasty made with caribou, elk or medium-sized goose breasts.*

| | | |
|---|---|---:|
| 2 tbsp. | flour | 30 mL |
| 1 tsp. | DLS* OR ½ tsp. (5 mL) salt and ¼ tsp. (1 mL) pepper | 5 mL |
| 1½ lbs. | moose steak, 4 to 6 serving-sized pieces, boneless cut, ¾" (2 cm) thick | 750 g |
| 2 tbsp. | vegetable oil OR more as needed | 30 mL |
| 3 | celery stalks, in 1½" (4 cm) lengths | 3 |
| ½ lb. | mushrooms, halved (1 cup [250 mL]) | 250 g |
| 6 | green onions, in 1½" (4 cm) lengths | 6 |
| ⅓ cup | red wine | 75 mL |
| 3 tbsp. | soy sauce | 45 mL |
| ½ tsp. | ground ginger | 2 mL |
| ¼ tsp. | cinnamon | 1 mL |
| ¼ tsp. | cayenne | 1 mL |

1. Combine the flour and DLS* or salt and pepper. With a mallet (the bottom edge of a wine bottle works fine), pound the seasoned flour into the meat. The meat should end up about ¼" (1 cm) thick.
2. Heat the oil in a large frying pan over medium-high heat. Add the meat and brown well on both sides.
3. Scatter the celery, mushrooms and ⅔ of the green onions over the meat.
4. Combine the remaining ingredients in a small bowl and pour over the meat.
5. Bring to a simmer; cover the frying pan and simmer for 1 to 1¼ hours, until the meat is tender when pierced. Scatter the remaining green onions over the steak; cover and cook for an additional 5 minutes.

**Serves 4**

NOTE: This teams up well with wild rice, a nice green salad and hot buttery rolls.

*\* Dymond Lake Seasoning, see page 3.*

# MINERS' STEAK

*This is an especially easy dish to prepare because the meat doesn't have to be browned first. Use any wild meat that is available. Tender and delicious!*

| | | |
|---|---|---:|
| ¼ cup | flour | 60 mL |
| 1 tsp. | salt | 5 mL |
| ¼ tsp. | pepper | 1 mL |
| 1 tsp. | DLS* OR increase pepper to 1 tsp. (5 mL) | 5 mL |
| 1½ lbs. | round steak cut into ½" (1.3 cm) strips | 750 g |
| 1 | large onion, sliced | 1 |
| 1 | green pepper, sliced | 1 |
| 10 oz. | can mushrooms, drained | 284 mL |
| 1 tbsp. | molasses | 15 mL |
| 3 tbsp. | soy sauce | 45 mL |
| 1 cup | beef stock | 250 mL |
| 19 oz. | can tomatoes, chopped | 540 mL |

1. Combine the flour, salt, pepper and DLS* in a plastic bag or bowl.
2. Shake the meat strips in the flour mixture and place in a Dutch oven or roaster
3. Place the onions, peppers and mushrooms over the meat.
4. Combine the molasses, soy sauce, beef stock and tomatoes and pour over the meat and vegetables.
5. Cover and bake at 325°F (160°C) for 2½ to 3 hours. Stir once or twice while baking.

**Serves 6**

SERVE over noodles.

*\* Dymond Lake Seasoning, see note on page 3.*

# ONION-SMOTHERED DEER STEAK

*Great gravy – great wild fare, this recipe may be used with all wild game.*

| | | |
|---|---|---|
| 8 | deer steaks | 8 |
| 2 | garlic cloves, crushed | 2 |
| | oil for frying | |
| | DLS* OR salt and pepper | |
| 1 | large onion, sliced in rings | 1 |
| 2 cups | beef stock | 500 mL |
| ¼ cup | flour | 60 mL |
| 1 cup | water | 250 mL |

1. Rub steaks with crushed garlic, then sprinkle with DLS* on both sides and allow to sit for 15 minutes.
2. Brown in oil in a heavy frying pan and move to a shallow dish. Spread onion over the steaks and pour over the beef stock.
3. Cover and bake at 350°F (180°C) for 1 hour, or until tender.
4. Remove the steaks from the pan and keep warm.
5. To make the gravy, mix flour and water to a smooth paste; add to the pan juices; bring to a boil and simmer until thickened. Adjust the seasoning and serve the gravy with the steaks.

**Serves 4 (or more if using steaks from a larger animal)**

*\* Dymond Lake Seasoning, see note on page 3.*

***Helpful Hunting Hints: Local knowledge and real knowledge aren't always the same.***

# DEER SAUSAGE

*Our trusty guide, Mike Boll, gave us this recipe. He uses deer meat, but we use caribou or moose. You try whatever you can get your hands on. But Mike claims that these turn out much better if you have a cold pitcher of Margaritas on hand when you are mixing them up!*

| | | |
|---|---|---|
| 12 lbs. | deer | 5.5 kg |
| 12 lbs. | pork with some fat content | 5.5 kg |
| 4 cups | water | 1 L |
| 6 tbsp. | salt | 90 mL |
| ¼ cup | pepper | 60 mL |
| ½ cup | brown sugar | 125 mL |
| 4 | large garlic cloves, crushed | 4 |
| | sausage casing | |

1. Using the course blade on your grinder, grind up the wild meat and pork with the water. (Mike advises that if you grind it too fine it will have the consistency of wieners.)
2. In a large container, using your hands, (unless you have a new cement mixer), mix the ground meat with the rest of the ingredients.
3. Using a sausage maker, according to the instructions supplied, make the sausages.
4. Package and freeze the sausages OR smoke them for a couple of hours first. See hot smoking instructions on page 45.
5. To serve, allow sausages to thaw and then either sauté until cooked through, barbecue, or put them on a baking tray and bake in the oven at 350°F (180°C) for 30 minutes.

**Makes 24 lbs. (11 kg) of sausages**

# HOT SMOKE METHOD –
# A DISSERTATION BY DOUG

I think a few words need to be said about the smoking process and the selection of the wood used for the smoking.

The method I use most is called the Hot Smoke Method, which generally means that the fire or heat used to produce the smoke is in the same smoker as the meat. The Cold Smoke Method generally uses a larger container and the fire for producing the smoke is outside the container with a tube or pipe to carry the smoke (without heat) into the container (smoker).

As we used a lot of cherry wood in building North Knife Lake Lodge, we had a lot of sawdust and scraps which we saved just to be used for smoking. We also import the traditional hickory and the more exotic apple wood, as well as using our native willow which does an excellent job, too. A mixture of sawdust and chips offers a fairly lengthy burn, especially if put in damp. As propane is cheaper and more portable at our lodges, we have converted our smoker to propane, with the burner from a small water heater. I adjust the flame as low as possible and set a pie plate or 9" (23 cm) square baking pan of sawdust and chips on top. Smoke sausages for 1½ hours. There is no need to turn them. Then boil the sausages in water for 20 minutes to remove any smoke residue, before freezing them.

*Helpful Hunting Hints: Never underestimate your guide. Chances are he knows more about his business than you do about yours.*

## Blueberries & Polar Bears – Webber's Northern Lodges, Our Most Requested Recipes
*by Helen Webber and Marie Woolsey*

Recipes for moose, goose and things that swim, introduce this comprehensive collection of recipes from two northern hunting and fishing lodges. There are also outrageously good recipes for breakfasts, lunches, appetizers to desserts, developed for easy preparation, using good, basic ingredients, acknowledging that the corner store is a boat or plane trip away.

| | |
|---|---|
| Retail $19.95 | 7"x 10" |
| 208 pages | 14 colored photographs |
| ISBN 1-895292-36-0 | wire coil bound |

## Cranberries & Canada Geese – Webber's Northern Lodges, Our Most Requested Recipes
*by Helen Webber and Marie Woolsey*

Fishermen, hunters and everyone with a love of genuinely satisfying food will be delighted with this superb sequel to the best-selling *Blueberries & Polar Bears*. Imaginative wild game and fish recipes are featured plus a new array of tempting breakfast, lunch and dinner specialties. Again, outrageously good recipes with easy preparation, using good basic ingredients.

| | |
|---|---|
| Retail $19.95 | 7" x 10" |
| 208 pages | 16 colored photographs |
| ISBN 1-895292-62-X | wire coil bound |

## Wild & Wonderful – Blueberries
*by Helen Webber and Marie Woolsey*

Blueberry recipes include Blueberry Bagels, Sunshine Blueberry Muffins, Blueberry Corn Griddle Cakes with Spiced Maple Syrup, Blueberry Crisp Cheesecake, Sour Cream Blueberry Pie, Blueberry Cointreau and more, even recipes for making your own dried blueberries and blueberry vinegar.

| | | |
|---|---|---|
| Retail $5.95 | saddlestitched | 5¼" x 8¼" |
| ISBN 1-894022-05-X | | 48 pages |

## Wild & Wonderful – Cranberries
*by Helen Webber and Marie Woolsey*

Cranberry recipes include Cranberry Orange Sour Cream Muffins, Cranberry Cheese Bread, Cranberry Pecan Shortbread, Boreal Forest Cranberry Brownies, White Chocolate Cranberry Cake, Cranberry Pecan Pie, Peach 'N' Cranberry Apple Pie, and recipes for Cranberry Chutney, jellies, juice and more.

| | | |
|---|---|---|
| Retail $5.95 | saddlestitched | 5¼" x 8¼" |
| ISBN 1-894022-04-1 | | 48 pages |

## Wild & Wonderful – Goose & Game
*by Helen Webber and Marie Woolsey*

Goose & Game recipes include Duck à la Orange, Jalapeño Goose Breasts Supreme, Spiced Cranberry Goose Breasts, Mushroom, Wild Rice and Goose Casserole, Wild Game Meatballs with Cranberry Dip, Sweet 'N' Sour Caribou Steaks, Red Wine and Garlic Moose Roast, Onion-Smothered Deer Steak, Deer Sausage and more.

| | | |
|---|---|---|
| Retail $5.95 | saddlestitched | 5¼" x 8¼" |
| ISBN 1-894022-06-8 | | 48 pages |

# SHARE WITH A FRIEND

$4.00 (total order) for shipping and handling

*Blueberries & Polar Bears* _____ x $19.95 = $ _____

*Cranberries & Canada Geese* _____ x $19.95 = $ _____

*Wild & Wonderful – Blueberries* _____ x $5.95 = $ _____

*Wild & Wonderful – Cranberries* _____ x $5.95 = $ _____

*Wild & Wonderful – Goose & Game* _____ x $5.95 = $ _____

Postage and handling _____ = $ ___4.00

Subtotal _____ = $ _____

In Canada add 7% GST _____ (Subtotal x .07) = $ _____

Book Total _____ = $ _____

DLS – 4 oz. (113.5 g) _____ x $4.00 = $ _____

DLS – 10 oz. (283 g) _____ x $9.00 = $ _____

Total enclosed _____ = $ _____


U.S and international orders payable in U.S. funds./Price is subject to change.


Name: _____

Street: _____

City: _____ Prov./State: _____

Country: _____ Postal Code/ZIP: _____


Please make cheque or money order payable to:

**Blueberries & Polar Bears Publishing**
Box 6104 Calgary South P.O.  OR  P.O. Box 304
Calgary, Alberta                Churchill, Manitoba
Canada  T2H 2L4                 Canada  R0B 0E0
FAX: (403) 251-9569             Telephone: 1-800-490-2228

For volume purchases, contact
**Blueberries & Polar Bears Publishing** for volume rates.
Please allow 3-4 weeks for delivery.